# How DNS Works.

Camboard Publishing
Cambridge. Great Britain.

www.camboard-publishing.com

Age range 11+

The Domain Name System is at the heart of the world wide web. How DNS Works explains how the domain system works through full color illustrations.

How DNS Works covers-
The early stages of the internet.
Internet protocol.
Uniform Resource Locator (URL)
Top level domains (TLD) and country code top level domains (ccTLD)
Domain name server.
MX Records system.
This full-color, fully illustrated guide to the world of the DNS, is ideal for computer science curriculums.

# How DNS Works

# Contents

# How DNS Works.

## Internet

In the very early days of the Internet, when just a few computers were connected into a small network, a method of identifying each computer on the network was required.

23.81.0.34

192.199.248.42

## IP Address

The IP address was born, the IP address consists of a unique number to represent each computer on the network.

206.71.50.203

Telephone
Line

Phone Socket

Modem

## Modem
In the early internet, each computer was
connected together, by a modem and
telephone line.

## Internet Protocol

The IP address, IP standing for Internet Protocol consisted of several numbers.
A typical IP address would be 203.11.34.143

## IP Address

Each computer on the internet, has its own unique IP address to identify it.

203.11.34.143

## Identification

It soon became apparent, that such a system of identification was not going to work, where a huge number of computers were in the network.

## Internet

Remembering different IP addresses soon became difficult and unreliable, as more computers were connected to this early Internet.

188.140.37.127

| IP Address | Domain |
|---|---|
| 209.73.186.236 | camboard-publishing.com |

## Text file
To overcome this problem a text file was created, that mapped names to the IP addresses.

## Network Information Centre
The text file was managed by the Network Information Centre, but it became apparent that this was soon causing problems.

## Internet
The text file was so large.
As more computers were connected to the Internet, it became difficult to manage.

| IP Address | Domain |
|---|---|
| 209.73.186.236 | camboard-publishing.com |

## DNS

A new solution was found in 1983 by the University of Wisconsin, who created the Domain Name System (DNS).

## Database

This new system is a database, that maps text names, to the numerical IP address automatically.

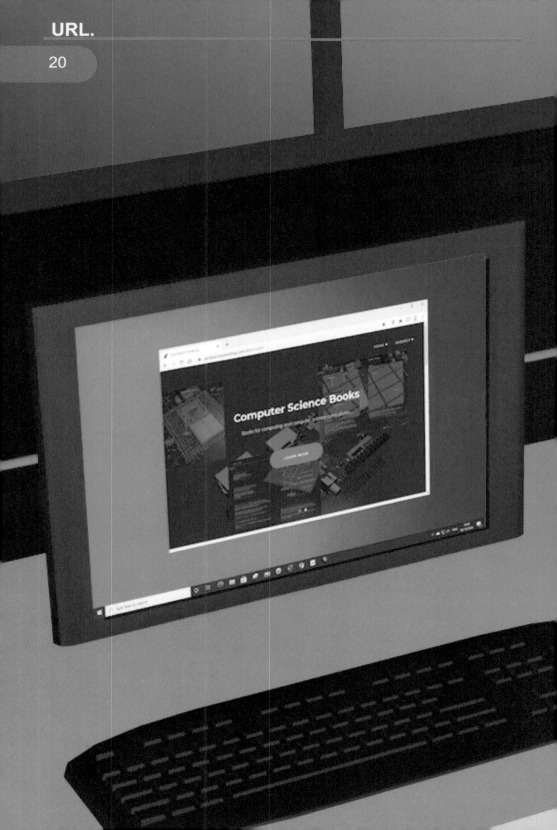

Uniform Resource Locator (URL)

🔒 https://www.camboard-publishing.com

**Web address**

With this system you no lon
remember the IP address, j
address i.e.-
www.camboard-publishing.

**URL**

This web address is the d
To find the domain, use y
browser and type in the U
Resource Locator (URL)
https://www.camboard-p

## DNS

Every time you use a domain name, you use a DNS to translate the domain name into the computer readable IP address.

## TLD

Top level domain (TLD) names are-

**.COM**
**.NET**
**.ORG**
**.GOV**
**.EDU.**

These are also called first level domains.

## ISP

Your internet service provider, will have a domain name server to translate the domain name to its IP address.

## DNS

The domain name server is a large server running a database with all the domain names in.

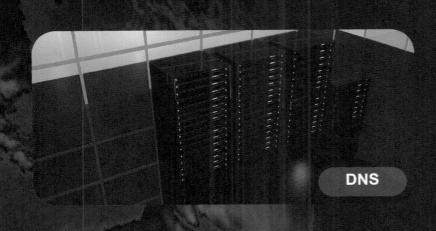

**DNS**

## Program

On the domain name server a program will run, that compares the entered URL domain name with a matching domain name in its database.

## Database

If the name matches, it will use the IP address thats stored in the database, for the matching domain.

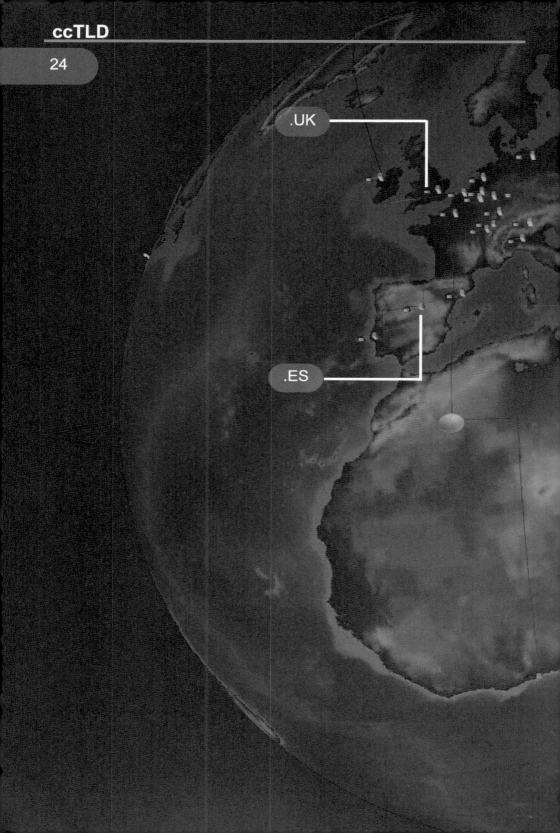

## ccTLD

Each country in the world has its own country code top level domain.

A registry in most countries is responsible for the management and sale of sub domains using its ccTLD.

Each country in the world is assigned a top level country code.

For instance the United Kingdoms is .UK

Top-Level name

https://www.camboard-publishing.com

Second-Level name

## Second-Level name
With every top level name there is a
second-level name, such as-

**Camboard-Publishing**
**Google**
**Apple**
**Microsoft**

Each second-level name is unique.

There can potentially be millions of host
names, providing each one is different.

## DNS Server

When the DNS server gets a request to find a domain name from an IP address, there are several possible outcomes.

The DNS server may already know the IP address for the requested domain, if it doesn't it communicates with another DNS server to find the IP address for the requested domain.

DNS Server

# Error.

## DNS Server
If this action fails, it can point the
program in the direction of a DNS
server that may have the IP address.

## Error
If all the actions fail to return a valid IP
address for the domain, it can return an
error message saying-
**This site can't be reached**

# This site can't be reached

Check if there is a typo in www.camboard-publishig.com.

If spelling is correct, try running windows network Diagnostics.

DNS_PROBE_FINISHED_NXDOMAIN

Reload

## Domain Name

If you purchase a domain name.
The register in the country that you
purchased your domain from, will have
a record for you to enter values that
connect to your website.

## MX Records

These are called MX Records, once
you have filled these out. The register
where you purchased your domain
name from, will forward these details to
all the domain name servers in the
world.

This means when someone types in
your domain name into a browser, your
page on your website will be loaded
into there web browser.

| DNS Entry | Type | Destination/Target |
|---|---|---|
| | MX Record | |
| @ | A | 209.73.186.236 |

Printed in Great Britain
by Amazon

34273959R00021